I'M MY BROTHER'S
KEEPER

DARREN BENNETT

I'm My Brother's Keeper

ISBN 978-0-578-76883-0

Contents

Dedication

This book is dedicated to my big brother, Shannon Santo Bennett. In many ways I cannot believe I am typing this, but your life was a life to be esteemed. Though 39 years seem cut short in my finite mind, you lived every moment of those 39 years to the fullest. You rose up against and above many odds. You served your community sacrificially. You supported your family faithfully and you loved people with an authentic, unconditional type of love.

I pray that through the honest and raw words written across the pages of this book, many people would come to learn a great lesson. I pray the lesson they learn would transcend your legacy, though I certainly aspire for your legacy to be illuminated through my words. My hope is that people can learn the lesson of unconditional love that reaches into the uncomfortable spaces of people's lives. A love that pursues people intentionally. A love that casts away all judgement and renders acceptance.

Shannon, that was you. You loved people that way. You lived with a sense of selflessness. You had this swagger and smile that captivated people and drew us into your world. Even if one did not quite understand your world, you had a way of making us feel loved, safe, and at home in your world. Big Bro, few people have that gift, but you had it! You lived it. I cannot personally speak for Jon Frey (perhaps, he will write his side of the story one day). I cannot imagine what he must have felt having you as a companion, doing life with you, and building a relationship with you.

You were the brother, one of five remaining Bennett Boys, who made sure you called each of us consistently. You made sure the family always came first. You kept us glued together. You would become upset with us when we strayed too far from each other. I remember getting scolded by you for not staying connected with the family more often. I remember you let me HAVE IT when you felt you had to "make an appointment just to see and speak with your own little brother!" You never minced words. Nope, you cut it straight. You came with the realness most people shrink back from. You told the truth even if the truth hurt.

You were that brother and uncle who made it a point to reach out to your nieces and nephew as often as possible. You were that uncle who hopped on a plane as many times a year as you could afford just to complete your "bucket list" with your nieces, nephew, big brother and sister-in-law in Connecticut. From Connecticut, you would make a mad dash to Jersey to visit your oldest brother and chop it up with him for a day. You were the brother and uncle who opened your home for me and my daughters on countless evenings for dance offs, sing offs, sleepovers, and whatever else you thought would create memories with my daughters! Not to mention the many times you shot out to California to see your brother, sister-in-law, and two nieces on the west coast. You did that, Bro!

You were the son who loved his mother and father with passion. A passion that cannot be put into words, at least not in this book. Though you had your differences with Mommy and Daddy on one level or another, you always loved them, and they knew it. You always made sure they were both taken care of as they grew older and more dependent on us. Yes, they both got on your nerves from time to time, but you still served them and cared for them as best as you knew how.

You were that loyal friend who gave his whole heart in every friendship you established. You were the friend who made sure everyone in your social circle received a text from you on a consistent basis. You were inclusive, and it bothered you if people you cared for felt left out. You were the friend who would give anything in the world to keep the "old crew" together forever. Sadly, everyone went on as life went on. Though it took a while for you to accept that, you eventually did. And you embraced a whole new crew, "THE BLASTICS, yawl!!!!!". That is a different book all together. You invited everyone you knew to your house parties and pool parties. Everyone showed up to your parties because they loved you for the way you loved them. Those parties were always LIT by the way (just puttin' that out there). You were outstanding in every sport you perfected, you were an exceptional partner at work. Anyone who worked with you had a WHOLE situation on their hands and will forever remember the day they worked alongside Deputy S. Bennett, myself included. I loved when we were paired on the same shift, in the same unit. That was a situation! I will say no more on that. Lol!

Man, you were the deputy sheriff who put on that Broward Sheriff's deputy uniform and your short five feet, seven-inch stature instantly shot up to seven feet tall! The community saw you as a beacon of light when you drove through the neighborhood with flashing lights. They knew you came bearing gifts for the children, be it brand new shoes for back to school or toys for Christmas. You served and gave back to your community. The homeboys from around the way in Deerfield never shunned you the way most police officers would be shunned in the hood. Nah Bruh, they loved to see you coming. They embraced you because you kept it 100! You kept it real and you showed love to the hood. They were our peeps! We all grew up together and you made sure they knew you had not forgotten that!

Let us not forget the students, from Lauderdale Lakes Middle to Deerfield Beach Elementary, who were impacted by you. You were the only School Resource Officer (SRO) who would engage in dance parties in the gym or cafeteria. You gave students a reason to respect police officers, even when the cultural climate of our time points toward the opposite. Many children today fear and disrespect the "po'lice", but not Deputy Bennett. Who could disrespect Deputy S. Bennett? Not many! Who could put on that uniform and command the attention of everyone around you? Not many. Who could serve the community so effectively? To the point you would die serving your community and become a legend in the process. Not many, Big Bro, not many. But you did all that. You did that. Long live the legacy of Shannon Santo Bennett!

Acknowledgments

Now, before diving any deeper into the emotions I believe this book will draw out of and evoke in you, it is imperative I pause and thank some very instrumental individuals. As a Christian, I must always give glory to God even in what seems to be the most difficult season of my 38 years on this earth. God has sustained me and comforted me through these very trying times!

I also want to praise and thank God for the amazing wife he has placed by my side. Christine, you are a phenomenal woman of God. The way you have served me and my mother during this most difficult season has been sacrificial and spirit filled. You have demonstrated compassion, care, consideration, and Christlikeness while walking with me through the many different emotional waves I have experienced.

There is no way I could navigate this storm without you. I am convinced that when God created you, he gave you every aspect of your personality to prepare you to be the wife of a man that would need a rock to lean on. You have been just that, my rock, my strength, my soulmate until the end!

To my mom, you are the strongest woman I know. To lose not one but two sons over the course of your lifetime is unimaginable. I cannot begin to think I can relate to the pain you feel. The way you have handled all of this has been inspiring! Your baby boy loves you.

Lastly, I want to give a shout out to my children. I cannot imagine how difficult it must be to balance the emotions and pain caused by the loss of Uncle Shannon with the strength and support you have shown to your grieving daddy. All five of you, in your own way, have blessed and ministered to me during this most difficult season. You have shown great maturity and character as well as hope amidst hardships! I love all y'all!

Introduction

AS YOU CAN see from my Dedication, Shannon had many great layers to his life. There are many levels to who Shannon was. This book will not come even close to shedding light on the many aspects of who Shannon was, so I will not attempt to do so. My hope with this book is to tell a love story. *Wait Darren, what do you mean a love story?* You read that correctly. Yes, I will tell a love story. A story of two brothers who were raised so closely together, most people thought they were twins. Two brothers who grew up doing essentially everything together from sports to social groups. This is our story.

My aim is the tell a love story of two brothers who lived in each other's world from childhood years into young adult years. Two brothers who eventually went opposite directions but found their way back to each other because of the bond of love. This is the story of how love bridged the chasm between a conservative evangelical preacher and an openly gay police officer.

That is my premise for this book. My aim is to highlight the bond Shannon and I had. My aim is to highlight the vast differences Shannon and I had. My aim is to highlight the way love kept Shannon and I together amidst those differences. My aim is to help others who read this book not only grieve with me, but also rejoice in the fact that love truly overcomes lifestyles. I once said to Shannon during one of our many in depth conversations, "I can still love you and not live like you." He liked that concept so much that he posted it on his Facebook page.

If you are looking for the standard "Christian" book, rich with deep theological implications you can apply to your walk with Jesus, you may be disappointed. If you are looking for the raw reality of two normal human beings who overcame their vast differences with unconditional love, then this just might encourage you. It may help you love more unconditionally. It may help you learn to be more daring about pursuing people who do not think or view life the way you do. Perhaps you are just courageously looking to step into a space of deep pain, suffering, lament, and heart ache caused by a pandemic called COVID-19. Well, saddle in, let us journey grief together.

Allow me to be clear. When I say I am a conservative evangelical preacher, I mean that I am doctrinally and theologically orthodox. More simply put, I believe the Bible is the inerrant word of God. I believe that in the Bible is found absolute truth. I emphatically affirm what scripture declares regarding the sanctity of marriage between one man and one woman (Genesis 2:22-24; Matthew 19:4-6). I believe there is only one way to heaven and that is by believing in Jesus Christ (John 14:6). I believe that hell is a literal place where those who reject Christ will consciously spend eternity (Luke 16: 19-31; Matthew 25:30). I believe we are all given the opportunity in this life to confess that we are sinners because we are totally depraved and in need of the saving grace found in Jesus Christ alone (1 John 1:9). I believe we cannot merit this grace by any works because Christ has done the work on our behalf. I believe that our salvation is gifted to us by putting our faith in Christ alone (Ephesians 2:8-10). I believe that Christ was born of a virgin (Luke 1:26-38) and walked this earth in perfection as the blameless lamb sent from God (Revelation 5:12). I believe Christ went to the cross to be our substitute. Christ died a death we deserved to die. I believe he rose on the third day, showed himself to his disciples as well as roughly 500 other people (1 Corinthians 15:1-11), and ascended back to the right hand of his Father God after 40 days (Acts 1:8-9). I believe he accomplished all the aforementioned so that you and I can experience everlasting life with him in heaven and upon his promised return we will rein with him on a new redeemed earth for all eternity (Revelation 21).

Just to give you a clearer insight into my biblical orthodoxy, I will point out that my theological framework leans very closely toward the solid and biblically sound teachings of theologians such as Martin Luther (not MLK Jr. No shade though, just clarity), Charles Spurgeon, Martin Lloyd Jones, R.C. Sproul, and Chuck Smith. Also influential were the teachings of contemporary theologians such as John Piper, Ligon Duncan, D.A. Carson, Voddie Baucham, Tony Merida, Tony Evans, David Platt, Joe Focht, and David Guzik. My personal biblical lifestyle, convictions, and ethos have been shaped by the phenomenal leadership of my senior pastor, Doug Sauder. Aside from Pastor Doug, I do not know any of these great men personally. Nonetheless, I admire the deep and diligent care they have given to proper interpretation of scripture. I have personally benefitted from the aforementioned men by way of their scholastic works which includes books, commentaries, and sermons. The works of these theologians have aided many young preachers, like me, gain a more vast comprehension of scripture that glorifies God, makes much of Jesus, and elevates the glorious Gospel. This biography of my orthodoxy will be extremely important to keep in mind when we reach Chapter 4, where I pose reflective theological questions that may raise the eyebrow of my conservative comrades.

My brother, Shannon was indeed an openly, unapologetically gay Deputy Sheriff. Shannon was 19 years old when he told us he was gay. Since that day, he continued to gain more courage and boldness to live life as a gay man. Even when he joined the Broward Sheriff Office (BSO), he never shied away from being honest when asked by a fellow deputy about his sexual orientation. Shannon's boldness was even highlighted in an article published on the BSO's web page for Gay Pride month. If I could respectfully put it this way, Shannon became somewhat of a poster boy for gay advocacy across the agency of BSO. From time to time, Shannon also performed in drag as his alter ego "Shanondra" and would set the stage on fire!

Shannon was not the consistent church goer. He did, however, listen to my sermons often, ask me deep theological questions, and seek out light, truth, and hope. Though he was fully immersed in who he was as a proud, unapologetic gay man, Shannon would never denounce or disrespect the name of Jesus. He would actually tell you that he believed in Jesus and that he had a praying grandmother! He would also tell you that he does not understand why Jesus would not just want him to be happy and find true love as a gay man.

Do you see the stark difference between Shannon and me? I purposefully, and in great detail, rolled out the tale of the tape between Shannon and me as to further build on my premise. You see, the better job I do at painting the picture of what could seemingly be a deep chasm of division between Shannon and me, the more clearly you will be able to see and appreciate how the love we had for each other filled that chasm and built a bridge that allowed us to freely walk into each other's world.

CHAPTER 1

You Don't Get It

HAVE YOU EVER felt like you were on an emotional island all by yourself? Like no one could or would ever understand the emotions and feelings you are experiencing? It has been said of this global pandemic, and I paraphrase, *we are all wading water in the same storm, just in different boats.* That could not ring truer in my world as I write this chapter. It is likely that it will remain true for the entirety of my existence on this earth.

What do I mean? Well, there are many well-meaning people who have reached out to me over the course of time after this tragedy. These people have rendered heartwarming and genuine encouragements. While the intentions are good, the worse thing one could ever say to me is, *I know how you feel, Darren*. Please read very carefully what I am about to express before offering words of comfort by uttering the phrase, *I know how you feel*. To be clear, I am not arguing that you are disqualified from ever saying that phrase. I am simply positing that it is unlikely that I will receive it as encouragement or comfort if you say it to me. As a matter of fact, if you do say it to me, I will respond in love and with a smile, "No you don't, you don't get it."

You see, I do not think anyone can ever really step into the headspace I am in and understand how I feel about what happened to Shannon. Just in case you might be interested in understanding, not feeling, but understanding what I am feeling, allow me to walk it out for you. Shannon and I grew up remarkably close. We were 14 months apart and raised by our mother as if we were twins. We did everything together, even into adulthood. We talked almost every day. I will share more on our bond in Chapter 3.

On March 24, Shannon texted me while he was hospitalized. He told me he was admitted and was undergoing testing while awaiting the result of a COVID test he had taken a few days prior. My response was to encourage him. But, I hurt deeply because I was not allowed to see him. We would text as much as he could tolerate before becoming exhausted; fighting to breathe as the days went by. I would try to lift his spirits by sending him worship songs and giving him an encouraging word. He would eventually text me informing that the COVID test result was positive. I admittedly did not worry much about the result because I thought, no big deal, he is young, healthy, and should muscle right through this. Again, I just wanted to see my brother and be with him while he struggled to breathe and even talk. At one point, he texted me expressing how terrible he was feeling and that he was extremely exhausted, and even afraid. I encouraged him to read Psalm 91 and told him I love him. He responded with the affirmative heart emoji. That would be the last dialogue I would have with Shannon Santino (I called him Santino at times).

I remember getting daily updates from Jon. From those updates I would eventually learn, on Saturday, March 28, Shannon had to be sedated, intubated, and placed on a ventilator. At this point I recall crying in my wife's arms and telling my wife as we lay in bed, *"My brother is fighting for his life, this is real, this thing is real!"* My church began praying increasingly each day, very intentionally for Shannon. The prayers for his recovery seemly were answered as Shannon showed daily signs of improvement. Reports of his fever dissipating and not returning were uplifting our spirits. Reports of his white blood cell count going back up and the pneumonia slowly resolving had me and my brothers prepping for victory. I recall texting Shannon, knowing he would see the texts when he came back to us. "You're doing it, Bro, you're coming back to us!"

Friday morning, April 3rd, my brothers and I parlayed our funds together. We wanted to bless the nursing staff for nursing Shannon back to health. This is how well he was doing. Though he was not off the ventilator, his dependence on it was weaning. As a result, we were certain he would be coherent and able to communicate with us again in the next couple of days. Was it childlike faith? Were we naïve? Did we misread the updates? All we knew is we were ready to celebrate. Jon and I were even making plans with the nurses to visit Shannon on Saturday, April 4th. Of course, we would take precautions and stand at his hospital room door. But no doubt, we wanted to go to Shannon, simply for him to see us and know he was not alone.

Then the call that changed our lives forever came through at 10:22 pm. It was my brother Joey on the other line. I answered the phone, *"Joey, wassup man?"* Joey replied, *"Darren, Shannon didn't make it, Bro..."* I could not believe what I just heard. How? Why? I kept yelling and crying, *"Why did you do that? Why did you do that?"* As if Shannon purposely left us. My wife and son tried their best to console me, but nothing was going the stop the shock or numb the pain. I could barely catch my breath. I almost hyperventilated. My head would not stop throbbing. My brother was gone! So sudden! This was not supposed to happen! He was supposed to beat this! The doctor told me that Shannon's heart simply stopped beating and they could not bring him back.

Once I was able to gather some strength, I had to go to my mother's "in-law efficiency", which is conveniently situated in my backyard. I would have to tell her. I would have to tell her that a second son of hers has died. She has now lived to experience the pain of losing two sons. This is not how it is supposed to play out!

I recall walking up to her screen door with my wife and son. She looked at us and intuitively knew. Before I could get in the door, I told her through the screen, *"Ma, he didn't make it."* She cried out, *"NO NO NO NO NO! WHY DIDN'T HE TAKE ME! I'M OLD, I HAVE NO LIFE LEFT! WHY NOT ME, WHY*

TAKE SHANNON?" All we could do was hold each other and cry. My wife held me, I held my mom, and my son held all of us. This is pain. This is our new reality. This really sucks! It really, really sucks.

The next morning, after sleeping for merely 40 minutes, I saw a BSO cruiser with its lights on parked outside my home. It was at that moment I would realize the magnitude of the change my life would undergo. After I had my coffee and worshipped Jesus (*yes, I did worship God for an hour after I awoke*), the Sheriff would have a news conference to announce the death of my brother. Watching that news conference on Local 10 News with my wife and mom solidified the reality that Shannon was gone. I am awake and this is not a bad dream. Then the circus began. The media circus. It now made sense to me how valuable it was to have the BSO marked cruiser at the front of my house. The presence of the cruiser, however, would not stop the numerous calls and emails I would receive, soliciting me to speak about this tragedy. My brother was now the first BSO deputy to die of COVID-19 while "in the line of duty." Yeah, it's about to get crazy, I thought to myself. And it did.

Many people can say, *Darren, I empathize with you over the death of your brother.* And to that, I would respond, sure you do! Many of you may have experienced the tragic death of a loved one at some point or another. Here is where I draw a line in the sand and place myself on a lonely island of grief. Can you say you know how it feels to want to simply grieve the death of a loved one whose death garnered national media attention during a global pandemic? Do you know how it feels to have your deceased brother's name and cause of death thrown amid a war between BSO's union president and its sheriff? Not even 72 hours had passed. I had yet to complete the funeral arrangements. Yet, I found myself in the midst of a feud between the BSO union president and the BSO sheriff. A dispute which started long before my brother's death made national headlines.

I will affirm that during these difficult times, my experience with the BSO sheriff was nothing shy of genuine compassion and sheer support for my family. The sheriff was kind enough to give me his personal cell phone number. He texted and called my mother, my bothers, and me consistently for many consecutive days following Shannon's untimely death. He even invited me to sit down with him and simply lament in his office, where he personally presented me with a large stack of bereavement cards received from all over the country.

Listen, I want to be clear and fair. I do not personally know the union president of the BSO, nor have I had any interactions with him. My intention here is not to speak unfavorably of the union president, but simply to express my thoughts as it relates to him. At minimum, a courtesy call expressing condolences to me and my family would have been appreciated. If not to offer condolences, at least a courtesy call to advise the family of his plan to highlight my brother's death in his publication. A publication which was geared towards heightening awareness around the union president's concerns for the alleged lack of PPE (personal protection equipment) available to frontline deputies, such as my brother. Had the BSO union president contacted me beforehand, I would not have denied him that right, nor would I have trivialized his concern. He is a union president doing his job and I find no fault with him toward that end. Had we talked, undoubtedly, I would have questioned his timing in the matter, considering the high sensitivity and visibility of my brother's death. Nevertheless, I never had the privilege to engage in that conversation.

I personally do not believe it to be unreasonable or unrealistic for me to have had that expectation. Perhaps in my emotional state, I am wrong. Perhaps the union president, as he put it in an interview on the local news, was not obligated to have a conversation or render a phone call of conciliation with family, who, in context, are "nonunion members". What do I know! Though I did indeed serve ten faithful years as a detention deputy, I am no longer entrenched in the standard operational procedures of BSO.

What I do know is, I woke up and there it was, the Sun Sentential publication written by the BSO union president featuring my deceased brother. A publication that thrust a knife deeper into the conflict between two men who had not just lost a best friend or a brother. The dispute was between the sheriff and the union president, but my family and I fell casualty to a war we did not enlist in. So, can you say you know how that feels?

Can you say you know how it feels to do an internet search of your brother's name only to find hate speech threaded in the comments section of the myriad of posts commemorating him on YouTube and Facebook? Oh yes, this hate speech came by way of people who have sinful disdain toward police officers and gay people, of whom my brother was both. Can you say you know how it feels to have the town of Davie Chief of Police make disparaging comments about your brother's lifestyle and spew presumptuous, hate fueled vitriol regarding the cause of his death? These comments, of course, reignited the media frenzy I so desperately wanted to avoid.

Can you say you know how it feels to mourn the death of a brother during a time when physical touch meant possible death by way of a highly contagious virus? Due to strict social distance precautions, I could not be consoled or hugged by neither my surviving brothers nor family members visiting from out of town nor friends nor my children who do not live in my home. My loving wife's embrace had to suffice and fill the void of all the other embraces I longed to experience in my grief. Can you say you know how that feels?

Can you say you know how it feels to navigate the cumbersome process of filing claims to insurance companies for compensation for our loss? Only to receive a letter weeks later from AIG (an insurance provider contracted by BSO), informing you that your claim has been denied! This thrust me into an array of emotions, as well as disappointment. AIG claims that COVID-19 does not qualify as an "in the line of duty death", per their policy. Subsequently, I immediately contacted BSO, who graciously filed an appeal on my family's behalf. After a couple of weeks, AIG corresponded with BSO, again denying the claim!

After deliberating with my wife, I did the very thing I dreaded having to do. I went to the media. I fully understood what this would mean. I would reignite the frenzy around my brother's death, which had already taken an emotional toll on me. I would put myself in position to be a sitting duck for the negative comments and criticism from the naturally born cynical people who live for the opportunity to posit their thoughts on the matter. I was willing to endure it all over again, this time to fight for what my family felt was right. My aim in getting media attention around this issue was to implore other first responder agencies who may be partnering with AIG to dismantle their relationship with AIG and look for another insurance provider. This would help alleviate any further disappointments to the brave men and women who put their lives on the line daily, particularly those who have an increased risk of exposure to this deadly virus. It would be quite simple and humane for any insurance company to modify its accidental death policy, in response to the fact that humanity has been rocked by a global pandemic.

Do you know how it feels to grieve your brother's death while pastoring a new, fast growing church as the onlooking community projects onto you how they think you should respond with your public platform? Considering all the aforesaid, I think it is safe for me to assert, you just don't get it. And that is ok, you do not have to because I am comforted by someone who does! Jesus is on this island with me and he knows. Hebrews 4:15-16 says, "[15] For we do not have a high priest who is unable to empathize with our weaknesses, but we have one who has been tempted in every way, just as we are—yet he did not sin. [16] Let us then approach God's throne of grace with confidence, so that we may receive mercy and find grace to help us in our time of need."

CHAPTER 2

Our Backdrop

I KNOW THE LAST chapter was pretty heavy from an emotional standpoint. Well saddle up. These next two chapters will take you on a journey, a journey that will reflect the bond that Shannon and I had for 38 years of my life. A bond that was unbreakable, a bond that was cemented and glued together by our backdrop, our history, our struggles. A bond that was mended by the life we spent together, the trials we overcame together, and the challenges we endured you guessed it, together.

So, let me start with our history, our backdrop. I dare not sensationalize our story as to paint a picture of two impoverished kids who grew up in a marginalized neighborhood trying to survive from day to day. That just was not our narrative, it was not our story. When I say we had challenges and we struggled, we did, no doubt. But I want to be honest and true to our story so that one reading this may relate and be encouraged that he or she too can overcome similar struggles. Not every story of struggle starts in a marginalized neighborhood or in an oppressed setting. Some struggles begin by the good simply going bad. What do I mean?

It all started when my mother and father came together to start what I would consider a biracial, blended family. My dad, who is African American, had two children of his own when he met my mother. My mother, who is Italian American, also had two children of her own prior to meeting my father. They married each other and created Shannon and me.

Our brothers, Joey and David are my father's two oldest children from a prior relationship. They did not grow up in the same home with Shannon and me. Residing at our home on 49 Travis Avenue in Stamford, Connecticut were my oldest brother, John and my older brother, Donnie (also known as D) *(RIP Brother)*. Then there was Shannon and me. John and D were a tad bit older than Shannon and I, so as you can imagine, they both had their separate lives. Shannon and I, on the other hand, naturally gravitated toward each other, considering we were only 14 months apart and essentially raised by our mother as if we were twins.

Now when I say twin, I am not by any means exaggerating that fact. We literally dressed alike every single day. We did everything together from the time we were born all the way through our high school years and into our adult years. If you saw Darren, you certainly saw Shannon not too far behind. We grew up with nicknames given to us by our daddy. I was Butchie because I was a little "tough guy" and Shannon was Boo Boo. I cannot recall the reason our dad gave him that nickname. I do remember Shannon as always being a little more laid-back, reserved, and timid in his disposition. I was always the more outgoing, mischievous, and rugged of our dynamic duo.

The first eight years of our lives, as far as I could recall, were very peaceful. We lived in a multi-cultural, multi-racial neighborhood. We never really felt as if we were different when it came to our skin color. I do not even recall asking why my mommy was white and why my daddy was black. We just were who we were, and it was OK.

The door of our home on Travis Avenue stayed open, as many of the teens in the neighborhood came in and out to hang with John and D. We used to be the house that threw the big block parties during the holidays. Everyone in the neighborhood knew the Bennetts; everyone loved the Bennetts.

One of Shannon's fondest memories of our first eight years growing up, aside from him sucking his thumb and simultaneously playing with my right ear-lobe to comfort himself, was the fact that we always sat at the dinner table together. My mom usually served some type of Italian meal, particularly spa-ghetti. My dad would sit at the head of the table just opposite of our big brother John. Shannon would sit directly across from me with D on his immediate right and I would sit to my mother's right. We would talk to each other at the dinner table. We would laugh with each other at the dinner table. Of course, like any family, there would be moments of tension at the dinner table. There were even moments of discipline at the dinner table. Moments when Shannon and I would have to stay at the dinner table for hours until we finished our vegetables. I can easily say our family was formed around the dinner table.

One my personal favorite memories of Shannon and I growing up was the many times we were called into the kitchen to sing and dance in front of our house guests. My mom and dad consistently had different family and friends over for coffee and donuts. My mom and dad were also very aware that they had two sons who were born to entertain! Shannon was the dancer! Even at such an early age he was able to watch, absorb, and emulate Michael Jackson. It was magical watching him glide across the kitchen floor. I was a bit envious but proud. Shannon and I were always envious but proud of each other, as strange as that might sound. I guess we wanted to be like each other while, at the same time, celebrate our unique giftings. Though we were gifted in diverse ways, we maximized our giftings to provide a dynamic duo of family entertainment! This dynamic duo of entertainment would last well into our early teen years, until we took up sports and began entertaining separate social circles. Yet, even as we fell into separate social circles, we would always look forward to coming home and reconnecting, telling stories about our day, and laughing ourselves to sleep.

I can recall being loved and cared for by our parents as well as our big brothers John and D. I remember fun family vacations to Florida and California. My father was in a popular and successful singing group throughout the 80s and 90s.

That was prime time for Shannon and me! We loved traveling to watch our father perform. We loved absorbing everything we saw on stage. As I stated before, we definitely loved when our father called us into the kitchen to showcase the fact that we had not only learned and absorbed the dance moves, but also that we could replicate everything we saw on that stage.

Shannon and I were grateful for music, because it was through music that we developed a special bond with our father. I am honestly not sure how much of a bond we would have had with Daddy had we not gravitated towards music. Music was my father and my father was music. There was nothing else, nothing more important. Do not get me wrong, he loved his family A LOT and he adored his children. At the same time, he most definitely lived for his music.

Shannon and I did, however, have a special unconditional bond with our mother. She was always very nurturing; she was the prime caregiver. She got us dressed, she combed our hair, she taught us how to take baths, and anything else you could imagine. I will guess we spent ninety percent of those early years glued to our mom. Where she went, we went. I used to love going out to different restaurants. It would be comedic to watch her get frustrated with

Shannon for eating like a little bird, as she would describe it. We both had a special relationship with her. She was our Mommy!

Then things dramatically changed. I remember learning that we suddenly were moving to Florida. Not too long after that, I remember seeing a moving truck pull up, boxes being placed in the truck, and Shannon and I getting in our mom's Cadillac for the long haul down I95 to Deerfield Beach, Florida. The thing is, neither John nor D were coming with us. My father was not in the driver seat of the Cadillac. He was likely sitting on the couch in his new studio apartment adjusting to his new normal. What Shannon and I had come to know and love as an unbreakable family that was a beacon in our neighborhood, was now completely dismantled. Our new normal was getting ready to take shape. Our new reality was upon us. Yet, as daunting as this new reality was for Shannon and me, there was this unexplainable peace endowing both of us. As a 38-year-old man looking back, I now know that peace stemmed from the fact that he and I were still together. Though separated from everyone and everything we loved and considered safe, Shannon and I were still Boo Boo and Butchie. And that was enough for us in that challenging time.

And so, it begins, the struggle! We are now eight and nine years old in a new state, 24 hours by car drive, away from where we felt the most peace. We are now considered single parent kids, growing up in a broken home. We are now in Deerfield Beach, Florida trying to figure out our new life. What Shannon and I would figure out very quickly is that "we were all we got." We learned very quickly that we were not in our utopia of peace on Travis Ave any longer. We learned that the words of my father would pierce our hearts deeper than we could imagine. Those word were: "Always look out for your brother. Don't let anyone or anything come between you and your brother!" Until that moment, those words carried little weight as we had no need to consider our dad's plea. In fact, we had John Bennett as a big brother. Nobody messed with John or his family. Oh, but John is now in Stamford living in a condo with his little brother D, trying to figure out what it means to be a 21-year-old with more responsibility than he may have bargained for.

You may be asking what happened to Mommy? You still got Mommy, don't you? Yes, in a sense, but she was not the same mommy. Something happened in that divorce. Something painful. I will never ever know the full story; I will never know all the true details. What I do know is my mother was different, she was insecure, she was afraid of failing as a single mom, she was desperate. We all have heard the saying, "desperate times calls for desperate measures." Well, that saying played out over the next eight years of our lives in Deerfield Beach, Florida.

Our mom went into grind mode to assure her two boys had what they needed. We did not get everything we wanted, but we had what we needed. She would work late night shifts at her job just to allow her the opportunity to be present during the day and attend all our sporting events, while still providing for us. She did what any good single mother would do. Shannon and I would spend most of our time playing together, singing, dancing, and trying to figure out our new neighborhood and our new life. It was in our new neighborhood that we had our first taste of racism. It was in our new neighborhood that we had our first taste of bullying because we were brown skinned kids with curly hair. In our new neighborhood, Shannon and I learned how to fight for and with each other. My mom just kept working and doing the best she could to survive.

Speaking of Shannon and I fighting for each other, I cannot fail to mention an epic fight he and I were involved in at Deerfield Beach High School, with a bully named Big John. I have no clue what his last name is, where he is now, whether he has a social media account or not, or if he is even still alive. What I do know is, Shannon was tired of being bullied by him. Shannon revealed this frustration to me, and my response was to handle it! I simply told Shannon that this John person will never pick on him anymore. The next day, as I was walking to class with my best friend, I saw big John standing at the double doors in our high school hallway. Coincidentally, I spotted Shannon in that same hallway. I immediately motioned for Shannon to come towards me, which he did, as he always would. No matter what he was doing, Shannon would never ignore me when I motioned for him at school. I then handed my backpack to my best friend and started heading towards Big John with a light jog. As I approached Big John, I cocked back and leveled him with a hard-left hook to the face! John immediately hit the floor. I began kicking his large six foot two, 220-pound body until I saw Shannon attempt to jump in. I say attempt because when Shannon tried to kick John, Shannon missed, and he slipped and fell! I still literally laugh aloud about that! Needless to say, Big John never bullied my brother again.

Now flash back from our teenage brawl with Big John to nine- and eight-year-old Shannon and

Darren. My mom would eventually meet and marry a man who presented as charming and funny at first. But what was unearthed in him changed Shannon and me forever. This man was an alcoholic racist! His antics and behavior had a very adverse effect on my brother and me. We saw things we had never seen. We heard things we had never heard. We were exposed to things no young child at our age should have been exposed to. Please understand, I do not say this to indict my mother. My mother was desperate and afraid. She felt deep in her heart that she needed this man to stick around for us to survive. She was blinded by this fear to the degree she could not see what it was doing to her, our family.

Over time Shannon and I were yelled at for futile things. We got in trouble or blamed for things that would cause you to scratch your head. We lived and walked on eggshells all because of this drunken racist we called "stepdad." Again, it was clear to Shannon and me, we were all we got. This went on in cycles over the course of eight years. Eventually, Shannon and I both became angry inside. We both grew resentment inside. This anger and resentment were sublimated into our athletic prowess. We killed it in sports to keep from killing each other and anyone that crossed our path. We were good kids, but wounded kids. We were all we got. We had dreams of making it out and making it big in performing or in sports. We talked about those dreams often. Our dreams drove us. We just wanted to make it!

Eventually, I turned sixteen and grew tired of our stepfather's verbally and psychologically abusive antics. One evening while my singing group comrades were over to rehearse, my stepdad was bothered by the noise and decided to protest. In his protest speech, he called my father a "nigger!" Hearing that, I immediately blacked out because of rage. When I came to, I saw Shannon standing over him laughing and yelling "Oh shoot!!!" I had knocked our stepdad out cold! My singing mates could not believe what they saw. Truthfully, I could not believe it either because I did not remember doing it. It did indeed happen. My mother, too, would become so frustrated that she threw our stepdad out and divorced him. So here we are again, much like eight years prior, just the three of us and we were all we got.

CHAPTER 3

Our Bond

NOW THAT YOU have read Chapters 1 and 2, my hope is that a foundation has been laid for the content in this chapter. It is no coincidence that this chapter is sandwiched right in the middle of this book. What you are about to read is, in fact, the bedrock or upshot of the entire book. Chapters 1 and 2 were no doubt vital to the building of my case. Moreover, those two chapters would serve as the thread that ties this book's premise together. The final two chapters, as you will soon read, will serve as the crescendo of my heart's cry and grief while navigating this most difficult season of tragedy.

So, what you just read in Chapter 2 is exactly why the bond between Shannon and I was and, in many ways, still is so extraordinarily strong. He and I managed to charter some difficult waters together, as we made it into our adult years. The key phrase there is that we made it! We both had dreams of becoming impactful figures in our respective communities and I would say, by God's grace, we have been blessed to do just that! As we became older, we would often have many conversations, be it at his home, over lunch somewhere in Wilton Manors, or just on the phone reminiscing on our upbringing and some of the challenges that only he and I would or could ever resonate with. We would even spend a lot of time laughing about childhood "codes" we created. Codes that we would literally speak in front of people without them knowing we were speaking in code. For example: "Sonny said nobody cares" from one of our favorite movies *Bronx Tale* or "1,2,3, ding ding" from *Rocky 3* or "I goofed it, I goofed" or "Just kidding, ooh ooh" or "Milk 'em, bacon bits" or "Not many" or "Congratulations Bro" or "Go to bed Joseph, go to bed" or "How can I look to my left and not see you there Bro" or simply just imitating our fathers antics. These phrases were redundant, funny, made no sense to you the reader, but made all the sense in the world to me and my brother! We understood and consistently indulged each other's strange humor. Do not get me wrong, Shannon and I had some knockdown, drag out fist fights over our years together. He would antagonize me like any typical big brother, and I would shower him with a flurry of flying fists as he curled up under a pillow and laughed. This became our custom as we grew up together, but make no mistake, it was OUR custom.

In other words, Shannon and I could fight each other and throw haymaker blows at each other, but no one else was allowed to lay as much as a finger on my brother! I remember recently reminiscing with one of our old mentors about this very thing. He recalled, "Y'all would practically kill each other but nobody else was allowed to fight either one of y'all." That is just how it was with us. My daddy set the bar and we raised it. I am my brother's keeper. That is right, we embodied that phrase. We fought for each other. We had each other's back no matter what. We supported each other. We were proud of each other.

As we became adults, fist fighting each other seemed to stop and our bond grew stronger. We just continued doing everything together, except for the fighting. As adults, we would have great debates.

Instead of fighting each other, we would fight for each other.

Now, when I say we did everything together, I mean that in the most literal sense. We essentially lived together in the same room as kids, teens, young adults, up until I got married and moved out. To close the gap left by me getting married, I helped Shannon gain employment at the Broward Sheriff's Office. There, he would excel in an amazing 12-year career. More importantly, we would be together again. That is when "bad boys for life" was born. I remember the amazing feeling of watching him successfully navigate and eventually graduate from the academy. I recall so many proud moments where I would show up to his academy training and he would light up with a smile. "There goes my lil big brother yawl", Shannon would proudly yell out. I remember watching him make it through his field training days and asking me for advice on how to handle certain situations. I remember Shannon coming into my housing unit one afternoon after asking his field training officer for permission to go see his lil brother. He walked in with his big smile and smooth swagger just in time to watch me show him how to handle a certain "situation" that was unfolding with a "pretrial detainee" that was in my care and custody. After the "situation" was handled, I remember Shannon calling me later that evening saying, "Bro, you're the deputy I want to emulate!" Well, he did one better, he exceeded my work ethic. He overshadowed my BSO legacy with a legacy of his own!

Man, there was no greater feeling than to work alongside my brother in that BSO uniform! We were a force to be reckoned with! There was nothing like showing up to a call and seeing my brother there. It gave me a sense of peace, knowing should the "crap" hit the fan, somebody had my back. The same kind of peace we gave each other when we went out clubbing or drinking. We knew if it went down, we had each other's back. We would ride together, and we were willing to die together. At least that was the plan until April 3rd, 2020.

I recall going through an exceedingly difficult season in my life, after failing in my first marriage. Shannon was right there to help me pick up the pieces and get me back on my feet. I moved right back in with him as he would counsel and console me through a time of depression and darkness. He would not let me sink. He held me up like the big brother he was. We would have long talks while watching TV together on his couch. We would order food and just eat and laugh at stuff. He even took me to get a tattoo when I was a little tipsy and emotional about my current life situation. I am not sure why I felt I needed a tattoo in that moment, but Shannon did not question it. He drove me right over to the tattoo shop and stayed with me until we got back home and back to laughing at stuff. Our bond was special.

Eventually, I would become more active in my new church and I started learning more about scripture and what it meant to truly "walk the walk" as a devoted Christian. This created some tension between Shannon and I because he had a very difficult church experience in his young adult years. That experience caused, what is popularly phrased, "church hurt" which created in him a bitter and cantankerous view of the "institute of the church." He had sworn up and down that he loved Jesus just as much as any "church goer" yet, I did not know what to do with that or how to articulate my position. The chasm was now formed. Houston, we have ourselves a problem. Shannon is an openly gay police officer and I am a conservative Christian with aspirations to lead in the church.

This would lead to many difficult conversations and even arguments. I must admit, I was not mature enough in my Christian walk at that juncture to navigate such conversations, so the chasm would keep widening and the tension kept growing. We still loved each other, no doubt, but I definitely could have been more sensitive towards my brother. Instead, I would beat him over the head with the few Bible verses I had memorized just so I could feel like I was "right." It has been wisely stated you can be "right" the wrong way. Oh boy, that was true of me indeed. I jumped up on a self-righteous high horse. Keep in mind, I had a limited understanding of scripture, but I was zealous for Jesus all the while misrepresenting Jesus with my zeal. Back then, we did not have memes to hide behind. What do I mean by memes? Well, these days, if one finds himself in a heated debate on social media and he starts to lose the argument due to lack of valid information to substantiate his position, he may simply insert a meme in the comments section. This serves as a deflector to the fact that you have absolutely nothing more intelligent to say. Well, my abrasiveness was my meme. In many ways, I feel I started distancing myself from him because I was not able to articulate my biblical position, which was in juxtaposition to his, in a loving way.

Even worse, I hurt my brother deeply by declining to hang out with him on many occasions. You must remember, we did everything together so, he was not used to this chasm. I did not like it either, but it was my "safe place." It got so bad that he and I argued about this distance I caused to the point that he blocked me on Facebook. Even more sad, I was actually happy he blocked me because it gave me more of an excuse to remain distant and "safe." Boy, was I a huge jerk! Shannon had frustrations, feelings, and emotions that needed tender care. Initially, I had done a poor job at caring for my brother's heart.

What do I mean? In Chapter 1, I expressed how I am on an "island" of grief all by myself, experiencing feelings that no one but Jesus would ever be able to understand or empathize with. Well, that is exactly how my brother felt. In fact, let me qualify what I just said and am about to say this way. I have not just one, but two gay brothers. My brother Donnie "D" (RIP) was openly gay and at some point, professed Jesus at Calvary Chapel many years prior to me becoming a leader there. Not only do I have two gay brothers, one of my life long best friends (still a best friend to this very present day) is gay. Knowing what I know now, by way of honest conversations with all three of these men I love, I can posit that most gay men and women have, at some point or another, felt like they are trapped on an "island" that no one would ever understand. Imagine having these same sex desires that society and culture consider as not normative.

Imagine wrestling with that and reconciling the desire to follow Jesus. These three men I mentioned have walked that daunting road. Trying to figure out why you feel the way you do, afraid of being judged. These three men would tell you they wanted to fit in with the "guys" like anyone else, but never really felt like they truly fit in. The truth was, as soon as an attractive woman walked by, their reality struck hard. While the rest of the "guys" were having googly eyes over the attractive woman who just walked by, they were low key admiring the googly eyes of the "guys."

Darren, how did you eventually close this chasm? Great question! I closed it by closing my mouth! In other words, I was willing to stop trying to beat my brother over the head with scripture, stop trying to "fix him" and in the process making him feel condemned. Instead, I tried to have a seat on that lonely island. Not fake like I understood what my brother was feeling, but simply be present with him, love him, and listen to him. You would be surprised how much one can learn if one practiced what the Bible mandates about being "slow to speak and quick to listen" (James 1:19). I began rebuilding relational equity with my brother by pursing him in his world. This rebuilding process did not just happen overnight. It happened over many honest and transparent lunch and phone conversations. We just put it all out there. All our pain, disappointments, and hurt we caused each other. We took ownership of all our improprieties toward each other and exercised the gift of forgiveness! I can literally remember sitting across from my brother with both of us in tears. Imagine two grown men having Mexican food, crying tears. And not because the tacos were spicy.

As I matured in my walk with Jesus, I started to more clearly understand scripture and the way Jesus operated with those who "lived on islands", so to speak. I was convinced and convicted at the same time! I knew I had a beautiful opportunity to share and show the love of Christ by stretching myself beyond what was comfortable. What do I mean? I no longer distanced myself by declining invitations to hang out with my brother in his world. Things had to change and thankfully they did. I now intentionally spent time at his famous house parties and pool parties and enjoyed dinner at various restaurants in Wilton Manors, a predominantly gay community where he once lived. While I attended his famous and always well attended house parties, I made sure what people saw was a servant and not a preacher. Ninety percent of the attendees at most of my brother's parties were of the LGBTQ disposition.

Did that make me the preacher feel out of place at times? Yes, a little. Did I lean into the opportunity? Yes! I served people. I stood at Shannon's front door and gave myself a job on the "welcoming committee." I lovingly greeted, welcomed, and hugged everyone on the way in.

Please understand, I do not mention this next portion of the story to sound self-serving but to emphasize my point. I remember Shannon texting me one morning after a house party he had. Shannon said, "Bro, Thank you." He then sent multiple screen shots from his party guests. Those screen shots were text messages his party guests sent to him. They were floored by the fact that a pastor would meet, greet, and hug them as they walked into the party. Shannon went on to express how loved he felt by me for the way I loved his friends, and how proud he was of his lil brother, "the preacher."

Guys, there is no secret sauce to this. It is literally taking on the heart of Jesus toward those who feel like outsiders. Take the Bible narrative in John 4 as a proof text. Jesus intentionally pursued the woman at the well. This was a woman who had a track record of sin. This was a woman who felt like she, "a Samaritan", should not even talk to a Jew. In that period, the town of Samaria was frowned upon by the Jews. Most Jews avoided the town and would take the long way of travel as to not enter the town. Yet, Jesus (a Jew) intentionally went there. Make no mistake about it, after Jesus built a bridge of relational equity with the woman by way of conversation, he did speak truth to her regarding her indiscretions and his ability to be that which she had been void of her entire life. He told her he would be her living water. That he would be the answer to the emptiness she felt on the inside.

Here is my point. We see this play out repeatedly in scripture where Jesus pursues and builds relational equity with people society would consider outcasts or "on an island." Eventually, I would build up enough equity with my brother to the degree that he would start coming to me with the hard biblical questions. Questions about God's hand in suffering, the eternal destiny of those who died by committing suicide, and why a loving God would allow slavery? These are hard questions y'all! Shannon was not asking me these hard questions to trip me up. He was not looking to validate his lifestyle or make God out to be the "bad guy." Shannon genuinely wanted to understand God. Shannon loved people and wanted to know why people suffer. This time the conversation took a different tone though. The tone was truth in love, not condemnation.

My gay best friend, who grew up in church, once told me that his greatest angst and disappointment with "church people" is the tone of condemnation. In his words, *"Darren, I grew up hearing that being gay was a sin. I prayed and cried every night as a teen asking God to remove my 'gayness' from me so the church would accept me. God didn't remove it, so I'm gay but I love Jesus."* He would go onto to tell me and my wife over dinner one evening how he still reads his word, still listens to worship music as well as good preaching, and still presents himself at work as a God-fearing man. He then threw us for a loop and a great laugh when he stated, *"Heck, I might be gay once a month if I can get a man to sleep with me."*

So, what do you do with that?!?! My best friend loves Jesus but has been hurt by his church experience. The pastor was not able to successfully lay hands on him and "heal him of his gayness." Now let me be clear, as my sarcasm cannot be expressed as you are reading. I was being facetious when I said the pastor was not able to successfully "lay hands" and heal him from his gayness. I do not believe gayness is something that can be cast out by the "laying on of hands." I do not think that is what James was referring to when he said, "if anyone is sick among you let him go to the elders for prayer to be anointed and have hands laid on them for healing" (James 5:14-16). What we have here is an issue that is a result of our "fallen" condition. God does not make mistakes, no doubt. But in his sovereign and redemptive plan for humanity, we are conceived in sin therefore, born into sin and gripped with pro-clivities that he would have us resist (Psalm 51:5). It is called same sex attraction. God may not necessarily remove that desire, but he will give us the ability to resist that desire. In our weakness he is made strong, but it is a long journey and difficult battle, no doubt (2 Corinthians 12:9-11). My gay friend considers himself a Christian who feels socially ousted by the church but accepted by those who have the same disposition as him. He and Shannon had a remarkably similar testimony around their church hurt and pain. He and Shannon were also able to build a bond around that pain. When I hear the hearts' cry of my brother and my best friend, it grieves me. When Shannon asked me the question, "Darren, why can't I love Jesus and still be who I am. I just want to be happy. Doesn't God want me to be happy?" With tears in my eyes, I would look Shannon in the eyes and tell him Jesus wants you to be happy. But more importantly, he wants you to experience true Joy. A Joy only found only in him.

I once told Shannon and my best friend that the thing that makes me different from them is not my sexual orientation or disposition, but my choice. What makes me different is my choice. Choice Darren? Yes, you see, we are all sinners in the sight of God (Romans 3:23) and we will continue to fall shy of God's holy standard until he returns or calls us into eternity. Christ, however, would be the fulfillment of that remarkably high standard of holiness (Matthew 5:17). In my gratitude for this unfailing love of Christ, I choose to see, savor, and treasure Christ as more valuable than the thing that vies for my affections daily. What is that thing you ask? Lust! On any given day I, Darren, the preacher, have the proclivity to lust, to fall back into pornography addiction, or womanizing, or alcoholism, or even fits of rage. All of which I thought satisfied my heart and impulses. Truth is that those things do not and will not satisfy me. Though they may temporality gratify me, my true satisfaction is found in Christ's love for me. The fact that he saw me as all those things I just listed above and still pursued me in my weakest and darkest moment of life and call me his son is overwhelming. That reality is what is most satisfying. That is why I make a cognitive and emotional decision each day to not give into the very impulses that I too have begged God to take from me, yet still remain. I remember one day walking across the parking lot to work, praying to God while praising myself. I said, "God, if you would just take my lust issue away so I don't have to struggle with it all the time, I'd be almost sinless and perfect." Then I heard a still small voice respond to me (in my mind, not audibly), that is the reason I will not take it away, my son. You are made perfect in me even with your imperfections! I wrestle daily with the temptation of my sin nature, but I do not take rest in my sin nature.

We are all leveled at the foot of the cross. My proclivity, my best friend's proclivity, and my brother's proclivity are all equal when we look up from leveled ground and see our savior hanging there on that cross in our place! I have told Shannon this. We have talked through this. I have told Shannon that "The Church" has not done the greatest job at making him and others who live on that very "island" feel loved and accepted. I am a pastor; I am willing to humbly admit that.

I have also told Shannon, as well as my best friend, that Christians should not throw stones at people of the gay disposition with their left hand while clicking on porn sites with their right hand, or clinging to their alcoholic beverage with their right hand, or abusing their wife with their right hand. You get my point? Christ asked the woman who was caught in adultery where were her accusers. She looked up and saw none. Of course, her accusers all scattered when Jesus challenged them. He called for those who were without sin to cast the first stone. To which they responded by walking away, leaving the adulterous woman at the feet of Jesus to receive grace and a poignant appeal to not sin in that way again (John 8:1-11).

These are the types of raw conversations I have had with my brother quite often. This is what it all boils down to for me, guys. I do not believe that we should bend or stretch the word of God to fit our desires or disposition or whatever culture determines is acceptable. I do believe that as Christians, we should do better at bending and stretching ourselves into the context of those with different dispositions than us in effort to love them well, as they grapple with the word of God.

CHAPTER 4

Our Bridge

S HANNON DID NOT have a problem believing in Jesus. Oh, he would tell you that while he was a believer in Christ (more details on that in the next chapter), he had a problem believing Jesus. It was cognitive dissonance. He could not square how he felt with how the word of God told him he ought to live. My job as a Christian was to build enough relational equity with my brother so that I would have space to share the word with him. It is not my job to force him to change or fix him; Jesus does that part. I am called to pursue and love people, the rest is in the hands of God.

Allow me to illustrate by asking a question then answering that question. Can a person who is gay and considers himself a Christian be a part of your church, Darren? Well, that is an honest question so here is my honest response. Yes. Let me explain to what degree. First for one to consider himself a Christian, one must profess a belief in Christ. Scripture is replete with this statement (John 3:15). Consequently, if my brother is standing outside of the church doors and says, Darren, I believe, can you let me in? Though I know he lives a gay lifestyle, he is telling me he believes. So, yes, I let him in! Frankly, I would let him in even if he says, "I don't believe but I want to come in!" Once he is inside, however, there are certain limitations he would have to navigate based on his lifestyle. Let me explain it this way.

To play on a high school football team, you simply try out for the team. Once you make the cut, you join the team. The coach then issues uniforms, shares team rules, and teaches you the play book. The point of wearing the team uniform, following the team rules, and learning the playbook is for unity of purpose. The purpose is to advance the ball forward into the endzones as much as you can to achieve victory. The moment a player decides to operate outside of the playbook, he risks getting benched and will be unable to participate in the advancement of the teams desired goal. The coach will then talk with that player and determine if the player should stay on the team. If that player fails to acquiesce to the play book, the coach will likely throw that player off the team.

In the same way, someone with a gay disposition can indeed be welcomed into the church building and church community. They would not have to "try out" or "make the cut" for this team though. They would simply enter just as they are! They would be unconditionally loved by the church community and offered the opportunity for accountability to the church community and taught by a book. A play-book (Bible) that would serve to advance the team's (church community) agenda, a KINGDOM agenda. If, for some reason, this individual has a problem with understanding or following the playbook (Bible), they would not be able to access the playing field, as this would disunify the team's (church community) goals and desired outcomes. The difference is, instead of throwing this individual off the team as would be the case with the high school football team, the coach (Jesus/Holy Spirit) would be patient with this player. The coach would sit with this player on the bench while the rest of the team (church community) advances the team's agenda and follows the playbook.

The coach (Jesus/Holy Spirit) would use the playbook (Bible) to help the player better understand how they can get into the game and advance the team's agenda instead of merely settling to cheer from the sidelines.

As a pastor, my job is to welcome everyone into the fold. My job is to teach the playbook (Bible) so that those who have come into the fold would experience a transformed life of delighting in the LORD. Pastor HB Charles once said, "It's the will of God, that the Spirit of God, would use the Word of God, to help the Children of God, become more like the Son of God." My job is to be used by the spirit of God to preach and teach the word of God. God's job is to transform lives such that those transformed lives acquiesce to his will (Playbook). Once that happens, that transformed life can make a huge impact on the field of play (mission field) and is able to help the team advance the team's agenda (Kingdom agenda).

This type of transformation does not happen overnight though. People do not just join a football team (church community) and become the star player or team captain (volunteer, community group leader, deacon, elder, pastor, etc.). This takes time, practice, and discipline, or as we call it in the church community, discipleship. This happens through a process called sanctification (2 Corinthians 3:18). God takes that individual who is sitting on the sidelines/bench and begins to soften his/her heart with the word of God. God navigates that person on the sidelines/bench through some "practice drills" (trials) that will help build him/her up to be who Christ calls him/her to be (Romans 5:1-5). I hope this illustration made sense. In summary, you are welcome here! I will teach the word of God here! The word of God, not me, will change you and transform you into who God desires you to be, according to HIS word, in HIS time, not mine. My job is to love you and pursue you with a Christlike love!

Let me once more illustrate what this pursuit looked like in the life of Shannon and me. As Shannon and I aspired to strengthen our bond irrespective of our difference in disposition, we continued to turn toward each other and never away from each other. Shannon made it a point to listen to my sermons and, from time to time, shared my sermon clips on his Facebook page! He would come to different church events and outreaches we would have. Oh, it was not just one sided! I did not do all the pursing. Once Shannon knew I was a safe place and that I loved him more than what made us different, the bridge was built! We both walked freely into each other's worlds with zero hesitation. Yes, different convictions, but same bridge. And that bridge was built on love. This type of love was unconditional, it was brotherly, it was a protecting kind of love. It was a love that flowed from both directions. It was our bond.

This type of bond allowed us to challenge each other respectfully. We, on many points, would simply agree to disagree. At times through tears, but love was always palpably flowing from both directions. It was a type of love that was willing to stand on a conviction yet, take a temporary loss in hopes for a greater outcome. What do I mean?

I remember he and I once debated about the gender transition of a child in pop culture. This gender transition garnered much media attention. Shannon did not like the way some people were handling the situation. He felt that this child was feeling trapped on that "island" I mentioned earlier. Shannon felt it was disrespectful that people insisted on referring to the child as a boy when the child preferred to be identified as female. He and I debated on this issue for a couple of hours. Of course, I took the conservative point of view. Yet, I was willing to pursue my brother and meet him somewhere in the middle, without compromising my conviction. I decided I would simply refer to the child as "the child." This might seem to be a copout in the eyes of my conservative friends.

I simply see it as being hospitable. In other words, I will embrace your position while still holding mine with the intent of having a deeper discussion on the matter and trusting God's word will shine light on the truth of that matter. My brother thanked me for my willingness to meet halfway. We hung up the phone, our bond remained intact, and we lived to debate another day. Well, we lived until the day of April 3, when our bond would take an entirely different shape.

Our greatest point of tension around Shannon's lifestyle and my biblical conviction was centered on his impending wedding. Shannon had gotten engaged to his partner back in December of 2019 and he was so excited about the wedding. I can remember him calling me very often to ask general questions regarding the planning process. He would ask simple questions that I could provide easy answers to. Questions like: "How much did you pay for the venue you used for your wedding?" or "do you know of any good DJ's that could play music for the reception?" He would send me pictures of him touring different venues until he landed on the perfect place. I never once felt out of sorts or awkward entertaining my brother's excitement even though the very thing that excited him went against my personal convictions regarding marriage. You see, as a Bible believing Christian, I still firmly hold to the biblical principle that marriage is a covenant between one man and one woman in the sight of God (Genesis 2:18-24; Matthew 19:4-6; Ephesians 5:33).

This is where things got a little tense. Eventually, Shannon would shift in his line of questioning. Eventually, Shannon would want to know if his baby bro is going to partake in his wedding. That, my friends, was not an easy conversation. That was one of the most difficult conversations I have ever had to have. How do you love like Jesus in that moment? How do you not hurt your brother and make him feel rejected by having to reject his desire for you to be in his wedding? Well, I will tell you what, I can only attribute the outcome to the Holy Spirit and Shannon's ability to reason with me. I expressed to Shannon that while I love him and want him to be happy and experience joy in his life, I cannot compromise my personal conviction. The questioning from Shannon got more intense. "Ok Bro, if you won't be in the wedding can you let your daughters (my nieces) walk in the wedding?" Again with tears in my eyes and compassion in my voice, I had to explain that as the ultimate authority figure over my children's life, allowing them to be in the wedding party would be tantamount to me covertly comprising on my biblical conviction. Shannon became quiet. I stayed quiet until I broke the awkward silence by winsomely expressing to Shannon that I would indeed attend the wedding with my children and take a front row seat. I told him that I would wear his colors and take pictures with him. I even told him I would get him an amazing DJ at an exceptionally low cost, which I actually did. Though Shannon was not totally satisfied, he did appreciate my willingness to meet him halfway on the matter. Now, I know there are some Christians reading this right now and saying to themselves, "Darren, how could you attend a gay wedding?" To that I would simply answer with one phrase, "conviction and compassion." My conviction keeps me from engaging in a ceremony that would stand juxtaposition to my biblical belief. Compassion tells me to show love to my brother by being there with him on his big day, with the hope of strengthening the bridge we built and the bond we have created. The conversation was difficult, no doubt. The emotions were heavy and tense. The wedding would never happen. Shannon died ten months before the set date.

What is the point I am trying to drive home here? It is simple, "I can still love you and not live like you." I said that during a sermon I preached last year on Genesis 19. One of the most difficult sermons I have ever preached, as it addresses the outcome of Sodom and Gomorrah. This sermon can be found on Soundcloud if you search Calvary Chapel North Miami. Shannon actually posted that very quote after he heard my sermon on Sodom and Gomorrah. That is how love really wins! It wins by pursuing people. It wins by building relationships with people who see things differently than you. It wins by being willing to take a temporary loss in hopes for the greater win. It wins by being willing to listen; be present and just listen. It wins by speaking truth in love and not with condemnation or acidity. It wins by yes, holding to your convictions while loving others through theirs, and leaving the rest up to Christ. After all, God is love (1 John 4:8) and there is no greater love than the love of Christ, who would lay down his life so we can experience true love. That is how love wins. That is how love built a bridge that filled the chasm between a conservative evangelical preacher and an openly gay police officer. That was and will forever be, our love, our bond!

CHAPTER 5

My Psalm

A S I BEGIN this chapter, I want to recall your attention to the introduction where I laid out my biblical convictions. As you read what is to follow in this disclaimer, it will be vitally important that you understand I have no aspiration to deviate from the convictions rolled out in the introduction. If anything, my faith and sanctification have grown deeper in Christ through this extremely difficult season. Romans 5:1-5 have been somewhat of an anchor text for me. It says, "Therefore, since we have been justified through faith, we have peace with God through our Lord Jesus Christ, ² through whom we have gained access by faith into this grace in which we now stand. And we boast in the hope of the glory of God. [3] Not only so, but we also glory in our sufferings, because we know that suffering produces perseverance; [4] perseverance, character; and character, hope. [5] And hope does not put us to shame, because God's love has been poured out into our hearts through the Holy Spirit, who has been given to us."

I have been telling people close to me I will never be the same after what happened with Shannon. I do not mean that in a negative or derogatory way. I mean it in the sense that God is making me better through this. He is shaping my character; he is sanctifying me; and he is cementing my faith in a hope for something much greater to come! So, I pray this chapter encourages you as I bare the depths of my heart and soul on paper. I pray you are challenged as I allow you to be a fly on the wall while I ask God some particularly challenging questions. Genuine questions. Not statements masquerading as questions, but legitimate hard, honest questions.

For those of you wondering whether I am allowed to ask God tough questions, I would respond with a resounding yes. God invites us into hard dialogue to grow our faith in him. Look at the book of Habakkuk, for example. The entire book is penned around the prophet asking God very difficult questions regarding a very difficult season. God responds to the prophet with raw truth that things will get worse before they get better. Nonetheless, God does affirm things will indeed get better. The prophet takes God at his word and worships God for the hope that lies ahead. That is how this chapter will be framed. I will indeed ask God subjective questions, but make no mistake about it, this chapter will end in worship much like one third of the psalms in the Bible. The biblical psalms typically follow the same blueprint of Habakkuk's book. God, why? God, how long? God, I am upset? God, I don't get it? God, I trust you!

Before we dive in, allow me to transparently disclose what has driven me to write this psalm is my angst for certain people and need for personal healing. What Darren? Did you say you have an angst for some people? Are you about to blast a group folks and call out names? Great question! No. I am about to be a human being and make myself vulnerable for the sake of my healing and grieving. Not so much for the appeasement people, but more so to help people. Let me explain. I have received comments from two spectrums of people, two perspectives if you would. On one side of the spectrum, I have been criticized for, and I quote, "not taking a hard stance against my brother's gay lifestyle and where that lifestyle can lead someone to spend eternity, which is hell." On the other side of the spectrum, I have been challenged as to why I have not made a definitive statement that I will see my brother again in heaven. This is to bring consolation to the hearts of the many who need to hear "me" say it. All this while I am grieving the loss of my roll dawg, my brother.

Well, let me lovingly, but poignantly, tell you that if you want to know the answer to where I believe my brother is spending eternity, then I would encourage you in a few ways. Invite me to have coffee so I can sit with you, build relational equity with you, and then help you understand how nuanced that question is and why I land in the position I land. I will not make a statement in this book because I feel the implications of my answer weigh extremely heavy on both sides of the spectrum. To take a position in this very public manuscript without establishing relational equity with those who demand to hear my position only makes me a sitting duck for the one-sided and uniformed views from each side of those spectrums. So, please do not become frustrated with me at this point. Perhaps, as you lament with me in this chapter and carefully read my questions to God, it will help you become more sensitive and understand just how nuanced this situation really is.

Well, here goes, my psalm.... God, this sucks! This really, really sucks! Why take my brother? He was young and had so much potential. Why take him like this? In a pandemic! He was supposed to beat COVID!

God, my brother said he believed in you. I heard him myself. He said he believed that your son Jesus died for him! He just wrestled with believing you. He believed in what you did on his behalf. Yet, he struggled with understanding what you say regarding his sexual disposition. That is right God, he believed in you, but he had difficulty with believing you. Doesn't your word tell us in John 3:15 and John 6:35-37 that "those who believe in me will have everlasting life" and "never go thirsty and that you will never drive them away?" Well, my brother tried his best Lord. I was there, I saw it. He knew he grappled with same sex attraction and he did not understand why he could not just be loved by you for who he was. Yet, he still tried God! He joined a church and suppressed his desires for a season. He was young and impressionable so when he and the pastor of that church had an unfortunate series of experiences, he was hurt. He was "church hurt" and he ran from religiosity and the institute of the church. God, you where there! You saw how he used that church hurt to then justify navigating deeper into his sexual disposition. Why didn't you stop him, God? If it was not your will for him to live that way, did you drive him away, against what your word says? Why didn't you trip him up, or did you?

God, he had cognitive dissonance towards you. He told me he loved you, would never renounce you, but he just could not understand you. So, he kept asking me the tough questions. God, I thought I was doing good! I was answering all his questions with scripture and in love. He was receptive. He listened patiently. He heard the Gospel comprehensively laid out. He responded, but he just could not understand. Did you blind his understanding and turn him over to a reprobate mind (Romans 1:24-28)? If he was indeed turned reprobate, then why, God, did he keep seeking out truth amidst all the sexual tension and confusion? Why did he not just outright blaspheme your name? Why did he end every text message after our biblical dialogues with the hashtag "prodigal son" (Luke 15)?

God, tell me! Was he a prodigal son looking to find his way home but stopping at all the bars and clubs on the way back? Was your calling him home bringing him to the point of his death? Did the "prod-igal Shannon" really make it back home? I just do not get it, God. Shannon called me his pastor. He posted my sermons on his Facebook page. He came to a few of our church outreaches and church services. He even asked me about becoming a member of my church one day and he would jokingly say he wanted to be a deacon. I would point him to scriptures that would help him understand why his sexual dispo-sition would limit his membership opportunities within the church "ecclesia", but would absolutely not limit the love our church community would lav-ish on him and his partner, Jon. Our church doors were always wide open to him and I dreamed of the day he would call Calvary Chapel North Miami his church home.

Lord, I do have a little curveball question to ask you. Why is it that one who claims to love you and believes in you, but has a gay disposition is imme-diately assumed to spend eternity in hell? Yet do we ever assume the same thing for a "racist Christian?" Can I consider a blatant racist a brother in Christ if he indeed claims to be one? I know many people that would. They would just say he or she struggled with the sin of racism. Hence, under that same prece-dence, could I have considered my gay brother to be a

"Christian" based on his known statement of "belief in you", as well as his searching out understanding about you along with his prodigal self-proclaimed disposition? Or was he merely a vessel of dishonor made by you to simply fall and fail (Romans 9:14-24)? Did he never make it back to us "the church" when he went out from us "the church" because he was never of us (1 John 2:19)? Was his claim to believe in you false? God, you know that I understand the difference between "struggling" with a sin and giving oneself over to a life of sin. I just have questions.

Why did you not at least heal him for me then, Lord? So, let us say you were not pleased with his path, why could you not honor my intercession on his behalf. You have been known to honor fervent intercession. You did it for Abraham on behalf of the righteous (Genesis 19) and for Moses on behalf of the stiff-necked idolaters you call your covenant people (Exodus 32). Am I not serving you well enough? What about the prayers of everyone at Calvary Chapel North Miami and Calvary Chapel Fort Lauderdale? Were those prayers not heard? Could you not spare Shannon on behalf of those prayers? Lord, I know you hear all our prayers (Revelation 8:4) and I know you bottle up all our tears (Psalm 56:8). I just have questions.

God, you did respond. You responded in the way you desired to respond. You ended Shannon's earthly life. But did you bring him home? God, if you do not answer my prayers the way I feel you ought to answer them, does it make you any less God? No! It makes me more human, fallible, and finite than I would like to admit. God, if you, for whatever providential reason, do not save my unsaved loved ones that I have been laboring in prayer over, does it make you any less God? Certainly not! Your ways are just and exacting and certainly higher than my ways (Isaiah 55:7-11). Wait, how do I know for certain that those "unsaved" loved ones who did not live a life reflective of "Christian fruit" were not mercifully given a "thief on the cross" moment (Luke 23)? Lord, that thief lived his life in opposition of you. He never made a declaration of belief in you. But the moment he was on the cross next to you, he knew enough about you to profess you to be the Messiah!

How did he know that? Did someone spend hours texting him scripture, encouraging him, loving him unconditionally the way you would love him? Did someone in that thief's life pour enough of your love into him so that he knew exactly who to cry out to in his desperate and dying moments? Lord, of course I would never recommend anyone roll "the thief of the cross" dice with their life. They would totally miss out on the blessing to experience joy, relationship, and fellowship with you as they navigate life. Rolling the dice, hoping it lands on Jesus, permitting you a conscious "death bed moment" to make a profession in Christ, is not wise nor is it God's desire? Yet, it has been done. Scripture proves it.

Lord, my brother spent five conscious, isolated days in the CCU on his death bed. In those days, my wife was texting him scripture and worship songs! In those days, I was texting him scripture and worship songs! My last words to my brother the day before he was sedated was for him to read Psalm 91 and I told him I loved him. He responded with the affirmative heart emoji. He would die days later. Did my brother have a thief on the cross moment, Lord? Did the prodigal son make it home? I have asked a lot of questions, Lord? I have so many more, but I will worship you instead. When David lost his son in 2 Samuel 12, his response was to simply worship you. The scripture tells us that David believed he would one day go to his son. I believe that heaven is heaven even without the loved ones we have lost because I have a hope that I will be with The Son, Jesus! God, I do not know the answers to the "why", but I do know the "who". Therefore, all through the night, I will worship you!

Lord, my hope is not hinged on my ability to ask you hard questions and to philosophically build a case solid enough to theologize my brother into heaven. That puts way too much pressure on me and way too much stock in my fallible theological framework. My hope rests in your character of love, grace, mercy, justice, holiness, and sovereign ability to reach my brother in ways I could not. Lord, I trust in your divine ways to have been able reach Shannon right where he lay in silence and isolation from March 23rd until his final breath on April 3rd. My hope resides in your prerogative to predetermine the very outcome you decree by way of your sovereign grace and will for Shannon's eternity.

CHAPTER 6

The Plea

AS THIS JOURNEY of grief comes to a close, I thought it would be appropriate to leave you all with some parting words. It is a final plea. A call to action expressed from a genuine place of love.

I just want all people to experience love and equality. I want people to experience joy and be at peace. I want children with special needs to be viewed as truly special and created uniquely for a purpose. I want those who are marginalized to feel accepted. I want those who are oppressed to feel freedom from oppression.

I want all the hate to stop. I want violence to cease. I want to see families spending quality time together. Parents do not just put your children in front of a TV screen or on a cell phone so you can sit idle! Do not take the gift of being a parent for granted. Create memoires. Create a legacy. Love your children deeply and protect them. Do not belittle or berate them. Be tender towards them so they know they are safe with you. Make sure they know they can trust you.

Start a bucket list with close family members and plow through it while you enjoy one another. Make sure you take time to visit those who live a distance from you. You have a phone? You know how to use it? Call and text your loved ones as often as you can remember. Put a reminder in your phone to text them. Just make sure they know they are important to you.

Throw parties and gatherings where people can come together and enjoy each other in a safe way. Truly value the company of your friends and make sure they know they are valued. Open your home and make it a haven of joy. Show hospitality and never partiality.

Be loyal to one another. Build lasting friendships that transcend proximity. Build bonds with those you love. Bonds that transcend your differences. Try your best to forgive those who hurt you. Even if you must forgive and love them from afar. Forgive them. Give people the benefit of the doubt.

Do not take yourself so seriously, because it is not that serious. Just enjoy yourself and the people around you. Take some risks. Do not box yourself in. Know your worth. Do not let anyone tell you what you cannot do because with God all things are possible.

As much as it depends on you, be selfless and sacrificial. Serve your community and give back. Find someone you can mentor or give advice to. Everyone needs wisdom from those who have been around the block a few times. Find a positive cause and give yourself to it. Make sure everyone knows what you stand for and what you believe in. Do not be fickle but find something to stand up for.

Be bold and courageous even if it costs you your life. Dying for a cause is way better than dying just because. Make your life count. Rise above every challenge and obstacle. Do not make excuses as to why you cannot do something. Prove to the naysayers that in Christ, you can do all things.

Make sure everyone knows you left a thumbprint wherever you were. Blaze a trail that others would be proud to follow. Live with integrity and honor. Be an exceptional employee and a dependable coworker. Speak the truth and people will remember you even if they do not like you.

If you follow this plea, I guarantee that the day you take your last breath, you will never be forgotten. I guarantee your name and reputation will outlive your time on this earth. I am certain that your legacy will go on even after you go on. Isn't that what we want? We want to be remembered, right? Oh, you will be remembered one way or another. The question is, how will you be remembered and what will you leave behind for those you left behind?

So, that's it, friends. That is the plea. Wait Darren, whose plea is it? Are those your words of advice as you attempt to close the book in some meaningful way? Is this what Shannon wants us to hear and give credulity to? Did you and Shannon talk about this "plea"? Did Shannon write these words himself at some point? Oh, considering that you are a pastor, perhaps it is the plea and heart of Jesus for humanity!

I am glad you asked, and I am glad you are curious to know exactly "whose" plea this is. The answer I will not divulge because those that truly know "us" already know the answer. The rest of you can ponder, pontificate, and hopefully put this plea into practice.

While you are meditating on this plea, I will simply continue carrying my brother's name and legacy into the communities he sacrificially served. I will make sure Shannon's legacy speaks volumes into the hearts of the family he deeply loved and always supported, as he indeed supported his family. There will certainly come a day that I breathe my last breath on this earth. What will be part of the legacy I leave behind? Well, I can sum it up in four words, I'M MY BROTHER'S KEEPER! Yes, I am! YES, I AM!

Resources

Though I do not personally know or directly partner with the authors of the below recommended books, I can tell you I have read their content and have heard them speak on the content within their books. I find what they posit in their works to be extremely helpful should you find yourself grappling with same sex attraction and trying to reconcile that with a relationship with Jesus.

Book Title: *Holy Sexuality and The Gospel* by Christopher Yuan

Book Title: *God's Design and Why It Matters; Rethinking Sexuality* by Dr. Julie Slattery

If you are looking for a safe place to dialogue about your sexual desires and your faith in Christ I'd recommend looking into "Oriented to Love" https://www.evangelicalsforsocialaction.org/oriented-to-love/

"Oriented to Love dialogue retreats offer a completely confidential, immersive, multi-day experience that helps Christians of all theologies and orientations/identities learn to live with and love the theological, sexual and/or gender «other»—and to do so within the context of a serious apprenticeship to Jesus. Beyond our shared faith in Christ, we seek not to find agreement but rather, through loving dialogue and mutual vulnerability, to build community in the church amidst theological diversity. We are able to do this, not by defining or sharpening our theological differences, but by encouraging each other in our relational commitment to Jesus and our shared desire to move toward him"

For those of you grappling with suffering and trying to reconcile where God lands in the grand scheme of our pain, I recommend:
Book Title: *Suffering and the Sovereignty of God* by John Piper and Justin Taylor

Notes

All scripture references are paraphrased except for Hebrews 4:15-16 and Romans 5:1-5 which are quoted from the New International Version of the bible.

About the Author

Darren Bennett is the proud husband of Christine Bennett and father of 5 amazing children (Destinee, Robert, Darionna, Darriale and Jael). Darren is the lead planter/pastor of Calvary Chapel North Miami a "live teaching" campus of Calvary Chapel Fort Lauderdale. The campus was started with about 15 people from the ground up in Darren and Christine's backyard. Calvary Chapel North Miami officially launched in April 2019 with 275 people in attendance. Darren has been in full time ministry serving in various capacities at Calvary Chapel Fort Lauderdale including: Youth Pastor, Children's Ministry Teacher, and Mentoring Ministry Director. Prior to the call to full time ministry Darren served as a Deputy Sheriff for the Broward Sheriff's Office from 2003-2013. Darren also has a bachelor's degree in Religious Science from Liberty University.

Made in the USA
Columbia, SC
17 March 2021